WE ARE ALL
GRETA

LAURENCE KING

Published by
Laurence King Publishing Ltd
361–373 City Road
London EC1V 1LR
United Kingdom
Tel: +44 20 7841 6900
E-mail: enquiries@laurenceking.com
www.laurenceking.com

A catalogue record for this book is available
from the British Library

ISBN: 978-1-78627-613-1

© 2019 Centauria srl – Milano
Text © Valentina Giannella
Illustrations © Manuela Marazzi
Graphic design Studio Dispari
Translation by JMS Books llp
Typeset by Marie Doherty
Cover design by Florian Michelet

Printed in China

Laurence King Publishing is committed to
ethical and sustainable production. We are
proud participants in The Book Chain Project ®
bookchainproject.com

WE ARE ALL GRETA

BE INSPIRED TO SAVE THE WORLD

Valentina Giannella
Illustrated by Manuela Marazzi

LAURENCE KING PUBLISHING

CONTENTS

For the young.

INTRODUCTION

It's Friday morning on 15 March 2019 in Hong Kong. My daughters' school chatroom has been buzzing since dawn: dozens of colourful cartoons have appeared, with slogans sent out by #FridaysForFuture sites. Today is the day of the great global student strike organized by Greta Thunberg, the sixteen-year-old activist and, because of this work, a candidate for the 2019 Nobel Peace Prize. Hong Kong has woken up to a resounding response from its students. Parents and grandparents are also getting ready to take the metro to Central Station, the meeting point for the demonstration.

'Mama, what does "climate change" mean?' eight-year-old Agata asks me. All children ask questions – it's their job, they have to understand how things work in the world. And now this diminutive Swedish girl, with her long braids and stern expression, has directed the attention of adults and her peers alike to issues crucial to the future of the planet, and the heads of the youngest children have been filled with questions. Global warming, the greenhouse effect, fossil fuels – what do they all mean? What are biodiversity and sustainable development? Who is studying the changes that are taking place here on Earth? Which sources are reliable? What action can I take?

The children at the junior and high schools have been informing themselves in the days leading up to the first demonstration, searching online, reading scientific articles and questioning their teachers. They have roped in parents who have had to study just as hard to produce easy-to-understand summaries for distribution in class. It has been tricky to pick a path through the fragmented information available from media sources and the concentrated data couched in specialist terms supplied by the experts, but they have managed it: youngsters and parents have been coming together in informative chat groups and posting summaries, analyses and answers. As they march and sing their way to Government House, the seat of the governor of their city, on 15 March, the majority of the students are better informed than the adults watching them from the streets and windows.

Just as in hundreds of other cities around the world that day, the children carried placards as reminders that we must act soon because, to put it simply: *There is no Planet B*. One placard in particular caught my attention: *My name is Greta*. It was carried by a girl with a black fringe and a steady gaze, another rather serious-looking individual, just like her Swedish peer. And it wasn't just her, it was every student at the demonstration, everyone who had studied what scientists have said for decades, who had got the message and decided to take to the streets because there was no more time: *They were all Greta*.

But this is not just the same old message, picked up by social media. It is not born of solidarity or of proximity but of a desire to create a new global identity. A fearless girl has awakened the conscience of an entire generation and made it concrete and visible: hundreds of thousands of young people sharing the universal principles of science, of respect, of the balance of the Earth.

This book sets out the basic ideas required to understand climate change, explained in a scientific and accessible way and drawn from the most authoritative sources. It is for young people and for all of us, parents and grandparents, who now find ourselves having to answer the direct and urgent questions our young people are asking about the health of our world.

'WARMING OF THE CLIMATE SYSTEM IS UNEQUIVOCAL, AND SINCE THE 1950s, MANY OF THE OBSERVED CHANGES ARE UNPRECEDENTED OVER DECADES TO MILLENNIA.'

'ANTHROPOGENIC DRIVERS [...] ARE EXTREMELY LIKELY TO HAVE BEEN THE DOMINANT CAUSE OF THE OBSERVED WARMING SINCE THE MID-20th CENTURY.'

FIFTH ASSESSMENT REPORT (AR5) OF THE INTERGOVERNMENTAL PANEL ON CLIMATE CHANGE (IPCC), THE LEADING INTERNATIONAL ORGANIZATION FOR CLIMATE CHANGE ANALYSIS

THE WHOLE WORLD AGREES: TEMPERATURES ARE RISING

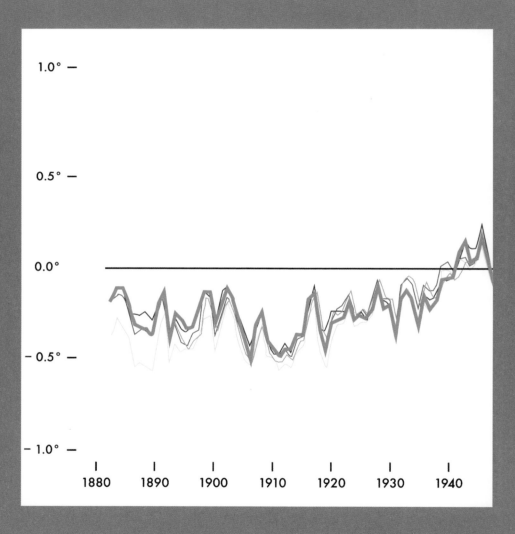

The sets of lines depict the temperature anomalies detected between 1880 and 2018 and recorded by NASA, NOAA, the Japan Meteorological Agency, the Berkeley Earth research group and the Met Office Hadley Centre (UK). All the findings show rapid warming, and every single one suggests that the most recent decade has been the hottest.

Source: Earth Observatory, NASA

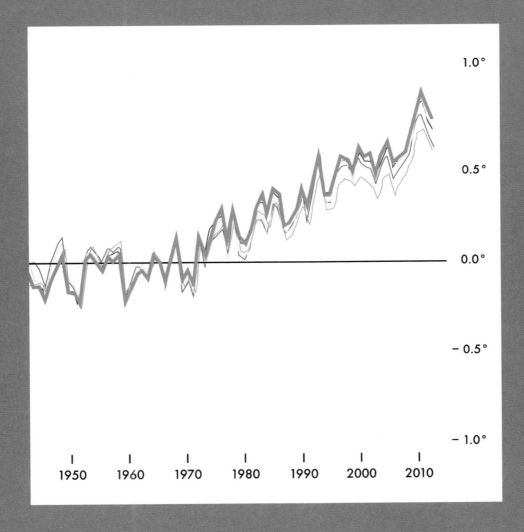

NASA Goddard Institute for Space Studies — NOAA National Climatic Data Center

Berkeley Earth — Met Office Hadley Centre/ Climatic Research Unit

Japan Meteorological Agency

CHAPTER 1

MY NAME IS GRETA

SWAP FEAR FOR ACTION TO SAVE THE FUTURE

Stockholm, Sweden. It is shortly after breakfast on 20 August 2018, and Greta is tying her laces and getting ready to leave the house, just like millions of other youngsters. Greta's daily routine is, however, about to change today. She is not going to school and her world (and ours too) will never be the same.

Greta Thunberg was born on 3 January 2003. Her mother, Malena, is an opera singer (who represented Sweden at the 2009 Eurovision Song Contest), a celebrity and a writer, while her father, Svante, is an actor. The Thunberg family tree boasts another famous Svante – Svante Arrhenius, who won the Nobel Prize for Chemistry in 1903 as the first scientist to examine the links between increasing emissions of carbon dioxide and the rising temperature of the Earth. Studies of global warming, begun in the 1960s, were based on his calculations in physics and chemistry. Entertainment, culture, science – Greta's background seems to promise a great future without a care in the world. But then something in this story throws a spanner in the works.

Greta was a curious child. When she turned eight, she began to wonder why her mum and dad were strict about switching off the lights, not wasting water when brushing your teeth and never throwing food away. She decided to find out more and started reading books and becoming informed. She discovered climate change and its consequences for the health of the planet. She was worried – she probably wanted to think about something else, but she had her own particular way of looking at things and she just couldn't let it go: 'If burning fossil fuels was so bad that it threatened our very existence, how could we just continue like before?'

The scientific bent that runs in the family and the support of her parents helped Greta learn as much as possible. Things started badly – Greta read everything she could find and the information clogged up in her mind like autumn leaves in a drain. She became depressed at the age of eleven, stopped eating and lost 10 kg in two months. She stopped speaking. Her parents took her to doctors who diagnosed Asperger's syndrome and selective mutism. Asperger's is a mild form of autism that does not interfere with learning or language, but instead often shows itself in single-minded dedication to the study of individual subjects and a lack of social inhibition in furthering one's own ideas. Selective mutism, on the other hand, is an inability to speak about things or with people if they do not trigger a deep connection. The only moments when Greta's eyes lit up and her words flowed were when she shared her concerns about the future of the planet: 'what are we doing to save ourselves, to save our children, my grandchildren?' Understanding that this was the key to helping her, her parents asked her to explain it to them first and then tell it to others. They listened. Her mother stopped taking planes to opera houses abroad where she was due to sing, her father drove an electric car and they no longer ate meat. The more Greta realized that she was able to make a difference, the stronger and more powerful she felt.

'We cannot solve a crisis without treating it as a crisis. ... We have run out of excuses and we are running out of time.' Instead of going to school on that morning of 20 August, Greta sat down on the pavement outside Sweden's Riksdag parliament building, a placard in hand with a few words written on the cardboard: 'School strike for climate'. The summer of 2018 was incredibly hot in Sweden, peaking at an unprecedented 35°C and unleashing wildfires that attracted aid from every country in Europe, including aircraft that dropped water bombs. Elections were due to be held on 9 September and Greta decided that 'if no one else is going to do anything, I will'. Day after day for twenty days, she sat in front of the parliament building. She began to attract attention from all corners. Her teachers were first, and they were divided between those who considered her behaviour inappropriate and those who came and sat with her, followed by numerous other ordinary citizens and activists, both young and not so young; and then the first journalists came. Twitter and Facebook broke the story in the virtual world and, within a couple of weeks, the hashtag #SchoolStrikeForClimate had gone global.

CHAPTER 2

YES, WE WILL

#FRIDAYSFORFUTURE
AND THE NEW GREEN NATION

'Instead of looking for hope, look for action. Then, and only then, hope will come.' It is November. Three months have passed since the first morning she sat alone in front of the Swedish parliament building and Greta has already taken the stage at TEDxStockholm (TED is an international platform that encourages the circulation of new ideas and opinions). With the zip of her blue sweatshirt pulled up to the top, she makes an eleven-minute speech delivering a series of key messages that will soon be shared across social media by millions. The most important message is this: let's unite.

'Be outside your government building every Friday morning. Ask for change to begin now.' To those who say that kids should stay in school and study to solve the problem, Greta responds, 'The climate crisis has already been solved. We already have all the facts and solutions. All we have to do is wake up and change. And why should I be studying for a future that soon will be no more?' And at the end of her first TED Talk, Greta reminds the audience: 'Some say that [...] it doesn't matter what we do. But I think that if a few children can get headlines all over the world just by not coming to school for a few weeks, imagine what we could all do together if we wanted to.' And so the new Green Nation is officially born in the ninth minute of this speech, and hundreds and thousands of students take the invitation seriously and set out to organize #FridaysForFuture committees in 270 countries around the world, linking up and sharing materials, information, slogans and requests. Greta was already the leader of this collective conscience when in Davos in Switzerland on 25 January 2019, she stood before the world's most powerful people assembled at the World Economic Forum and, without showing a trace of fear, reiterated: 'I want you to panic, I want you to feel the fear I feel every day.' The delegates listen, someone suggests taking notes (not without a hint of embarrassment). Her calm and authority win over Christine Lagarde, Managing Director of the International Monetary Fund, who fired off a tweet: 'Young people: keep pushing us to do the right thing'.

The first global strike on Friday 15 March saw 1.6 million students take to the streets in 1,700 cities around the world. Images of peaceful, colourful protests, from Melbourne to San Francisco, appear on the timelines of Greta's Facebook, Twitter and Instagram pages. Young people became organized in school and further afield, with many having read the summary of the most recent report issued by the Intergovernmental Panel on Climate Change (IPCC), the body delegated by the United Nations (UN) to study climate change. The report explains how restricting the limit of global warming to 1.5°C *may* be enough to help avert its most severe consequences.

Stock-market analysts have long since identified the potential of environmental concerns to disrupt global markets. In 2011, Milo Cress, a nine-year-old American boy, started an online campaign against plastic straws (Be Straw Free), forcing Starbucks and McDonald's to take action. Human consumption of protected species (such as shark fins in China) has also declined steeply over the last six years, thanks to awareness campaigns (such as those conducted by young people in Hong Kong schools). As Greta has reminded us: 'What we can do in our own small way, is always useful – if we do it together, it can have great results.'

The word 'responsibility' has been extremely important in mobilizing the Green Nation, inspiring not only those in power, who 'have to institute unpopular measures immediately', but also individual citizens. Greta's example of getting totally involved and transforming her fear and concern into campaigning for change sent a very precise message: #ClimateAction has also turned into #MyClimateAction. This trend answers the question raised by Hoesung Lee, the chair of the IPCC: 'Limiting warming to $1.5\,^{\circ}$C is possible in terms of physics; the technology and techniques are there; the question is whether people and societies will support politicians in taking these measures.'

Young people's answer is yes, we will.

CHAPTER 3

SCIENCE

A HOUSE ON FIRE:
THE GREENHOUSE EFFECT

Pricking the collective conscience invariably has an effect on public opinion. It can be positive, as it sparks an urgent need to know more about the issue and to do something, but it can also be negative. After that Friday 15 March, when images of Greta's yellow raincoat and the streets teeming with young people were splashed across front pages around the world, a lot of people began to wonder who was behind it all. Then the surprise came – there is nothing more suspicious behind Greta than thirty years of science.

The United Nations Conference on the Human Environment, the first major conference on the environment, was held in Stockholm in 1972. In 1987, the countries of the United Nations decided that it was a worthwhile enterprise to understand what was happening to the planet. The global economy was based mainly on the use of fossil fuels (organic substances extracted from the ground, where they had formed millions of years previously) such as oil, coal and natural gas. When burned, these substances produce waste chemicals that remain trapped within the atmosphere. One of these chemicals, carbon dioxide or CO_2, has a very special characteristic: it allows radiation from the sun to enter the atmosphere, but it traps the heat emitted by the Earth, warming both the atmosphere and the surface of the planet. This mechanism, discovered in 1824 by the French physicist and mathematician Joseph Fourier, is known as the 'greenhouse effect'. In the early 1900s, Greta's ancestor, Nobel Prize-winning scientist Svante Arrhenius, even calculated what might happen if carbon dioxide in the atmosphere were to increase; he deduced that temperatures on the Earth's surface would indeed go up – as Fourier had worked out in the previous century.

The World Meteorological Organization and the governments of the United Nations teamed up at the end of the 1980s to create the Intergovernmental Panel on Climate Change (IPCC), an institution that monitors and studies the world's climate and takes stock of the situation every five or six years. Their mission was to 'understand the scientific basis of risk of human-induced climate change'. The IPCC does not conduct research itself but evaluates it, cross-checking all the variables, outcomes and possibilities before producing a report that represents the facts as far as they are known. More than 2,000 experts from 80 developed and developing countries meet periodically to carry out this task, producing up to 150,000 reviews and comments on the latest research. You know the famous 'double check', the second look that is used in critical situations to avoid human error? Here it is, multiplied by 150,000. So when an IPCC report comes out, we can safely consider it to be reliable and authoritative.

Greta quoted the most recent special report, *Global Warming of 1.5 °C* in one of her speeches, saying: 'According to the IPCC, we are less than twelve years away from ... a disaster of unspoken sufferings for enormous numbers of people.' If we continue to burn fossil fuels at this rate, even taking into account the policies that have already been approved for reducing emissions, the Earth could warm up by 3 °C by the end of this century. Scientists think that such a temperature rise would result in the disappearance of surface ice for at least six months of the year, with all the climatic upheaval that would result: rising sea levels, drought, extinction of thousands of animal and plant species, and panic.

How can we put out what Greta has called a 'house on fire'? The IPCC goes on to state that the carbon dioxide balance – the difference between the CO_2 levels produced by the planet and the amount removed by natural filters (in other words, plants) or new technologies – has to be zero by 2050. This is absolutely necessary for limiting warming to $1.5\,°C$ above the readings recorded before the Industrial Revolution – and it is still possible. We must ask governments to reduce carbon dioxide emissions and to follow the sustainable development agenda designed by the UN to meet the targets set by scientists. Above all, however, we should be asking ourselves what we can do right now.

Over the next few chapters, we shall try to understand sustainable development, and we shall introduce the hashtag #MyClimateAction, to explore the options for acting personally. Don't be afraid that there are only a few of us, or that we are small: Greta was too.

CHAPTER 4
CLIMATE CHANGE

WHAT DIFFERENCE CAN HALF A DEGREE MAKE IN 80 YEARS?

The seas are threatening to rise by a metre by 2100, and young people are beginning to rise up too, taking up a strong position to combat climate change. They have learned a great deal, often at school, from well-informed teachers, from the mainstream media that has grasped the issue, and lately from online sources created in the wake of #FridaysForFuture.

When you read the last IPCC special report (which is also the principal source for Greta's research), what the committees of experts have to say might seem complex, but the meaning is clear. If we continue to emit the same quantities of carbon dioxide into the atmosphere at the same rate as we currently do, Earth may become at least three degrees warmer than pre-industrial levels by the end of this century.

Warming of this magnitude may well cause extreme climate change; half of the Amazon's 5.5 million square kilometres could disappear, and some regions of the world would be ravaged by heatwaves far more frequently than today, while others would suffer a greater number of typhoons and other destructive weather events – as is already happening in Southeast Asia. Drought, flooding and rising sea levels would force millions of humans living in coastal areas around the world – not to mention entire nations, such as the Maldives – to migrate from islands, shores and estuaries.

The Paris Agreement, which was adopted in December 2015 and came into force at the end of 2016, was signed by 195 countries and says that a sufficient number of policies to reduce carbon dioxide emissions will be put in place by 2020 to ensure that global warming does not exceed the required limit of 2 °C above pre-industrial levels by 2100; it also recommends an ideal level of 1.5 °C. Why is this? What difference could half a degree less of warming make? The IPCC had the job of explaining, and in October 2018 established that it would make a huge difference. **If we keep global warming to a maximum level of 1.5 °C, we could reduce the vulnerability of natural and human systems.** In other words: overall damage would be far more limited than with an increase of even 2 °C. And if we are wise enough to prevent this damage, we will have greater capacity to adapt.

WHAT IS THE DIFFERENCE BETWEEN WEATHER AND CLIMATE?

Weather is the state of the atmosphere at any given place and time: 'It's raining in London today.' Climate is the entire set of meteorological and environmental conditions that characterize a geographical region, defined over long periods (at least thirty years). The climate may be represented by the average temperature, for example, or by the typical range within which the temperature might vary: 'The climate of this city is mild.'

WHAT DOES CLIMATE CHANGE MEAN?

According to the World Meteorological Organization (WMO), climate change is the variation in the average state of the climate and/or its variability (discounting extreme events) over an extended period (thirty years or more); this may involve global warming or cooling. The climate change we are witnessing throughout the world is a set of phenomena that scientists attribute to global warming and which is in part anthropogenic (caused by human activity). Compared to the period before the Industrial Revolution (which began in the late 1700s), the temperature of the planet has already risen by 1 °C and could reach +3–5° by 2100 if we do not act immediately and decisively to deal with carbon dioxide emissions.

WHAT ARE THE MAIN EFFECTS OF CLIMATE CHANGE?

A rise in average temperatures and sea levels on Earth, increases in rainfall in some areas and drought elsewhere. Changes in habitat and the extinction of species of plants, animals, birds and insects. Increased poverty and hunger and greater economic disparity between nations. Mass migration.

HOW CAN WE STOP IT?

Scientists say that we should aim to achieve zero carbon emissions by 2030. In other words, we should immediately reduce our use of fossil fuels until emissions are equal to the total amount of carbon dioxide absorbed within the atmosphere by forests and technological systems used to 'capture' CO_2.

WHAT IS REQUIRED TO REDUCE CARBON EMISSIONS?

Reduce fossil fuel use. We need highly restrictive laws against the use of fossil fuels, combined with investment (both public and private) in new technologies that can make and distribute renewable energy. Changes in popular habits on a global scale; reducing consumption, saving energy, choosing food that is produced responsibly and traded fairly. Once a reduction in emissions has been secured, we need to work together on the sustainable development plan already drawn up by the United Nations with a view to eradicating poverty throughout the world. The social and economic wellbeing of the entire planet is necessary for environmental protection.

HOW MUCH TIME DO WE HAVE?

We should start reducing emissions immediately, at a steady and constant rate. The more time we waste making provisional decisions that are insufficient to achieve this goal, the more difficult it will become to counter the progress of the temperature beyond $+1.5\,^{\circ}C$. It will be both more complex and more expensive, with the added risk that countries in the developing world will find it difficult to keep up with richer countries.

RESILIENT CITY

CHAPTER 5

THE STRONG AND THE WEAK

RESILIENCE: MAKING SURE WE ARE READY FOR THE CLIMATE EMERGENCY

Typhoon Mangkhut hit the island of Luzon in the Philippines with a record-breaking force of 250 km/h on Friday 14 September 2018. Two days later, it had finally run its course in Hong Kong and Taishan in southern China. The sea rose by 4 metres in Hong Kong over a matter of hours, swallowing entire beaches – including seaside resorts – and throwing boats onto roads. The wind made skyscrapers sway, uprooted thousands of trees and knocked over a crane. The former British colony's Meteorological Observatory called it 'the most extreme event the city had ever witnessed in terms of intensity and damage'. Eighteen hours after the storm's peak, Hong Kong had already got its trains and metro back on track, the airport was running and public buildings had been inspected. Civil defence staff had cleared the main roads, and offices and schools reopened 24 hours later. There were a few casualties among those who failed to pay attention to the advice widely broadcast on every medium from TV to mobile phones, but no one was seriously injured.

The landslides and flooding that followed the typhoon in the Philippines continued to claim victims and obstruct activities in the region for weeks afterwards. The trauma was so great that the government requested that the name Mangkhut be removed from the list meteorologists use to designate typhoons; it was better to forget.

Mangkhut caused more than two hundred deaths in the Philippines, six in China and none in Hong Kong, and these few headlines sum up what climatologists (climate scientists) mean by resilience and its opposite, vulnerability.

Resilience is an area's capacity to stand up to natural phenomena. Resilient localities can implement action plans and organize infrastructure to protect the population, the environment and its various functions from events related to climate change. To combat these negative effects, we not only have to tackle the principal causes (the 'mitigation' that scientists talk about) but also work on our ability to overcome crises ('adaptation') and prepare the area to resist natural shocks.

Climate change does not manifest itself in the same way in every area on Earth. Scientists have identified several 'hot spots', areas that are already suffering, and will continue to suffer, the greatest impact. These include the Arctic, the Amazon, parts of Indonesia and Central/East Asia, and also the Mediterranean. You need only consider how great the effect of melting Arctic ice sheets can be during seasons with periods of extreme temperatures, as has been emphasized by the European Environment Agency (EEA). And then there is Africa; in addition to war in some countries, drought and flooding caused by deforestation and climate change have triggered mass migration, a phenomenon that is putting immense strain on Europe's social system.

WHAT MUST A COUNTRY DO TO BUILD UP ITS RESILIENCE?

It must invest heavily in:

1. Preventing the symptoms of climate change, which may be extreme events that strike rapidly (such as flooding), or long-term gradual change (such as coastal erosion caused by rising sea levels);

2. Warning systems to maintain high levels of alertness and to forecast potentially dangerous events;

3. Robust infrastructure that allows people to live safely even during extreme climatic events;

4. Renewable energy sources to keep emissions low and guarantee independence from fluctuations in the price and availability of fossil fuels;

5. Education, research and innovation to ensure that we are always ready to face up to change.

CHAPTER 6

SUSTAINABLE DEVELOPMENT

THE BRIDGE
THAT WILL SAVE US

Let's imagine for a moment that solving the problem of climate change is like crossing a river with a very strong current without being washed away or falling in. We first need to stem the flow, drastically lowering the level and power of the water. We then need to quickly place a line of rocks along the bottom, one after the other, to form a safe walkway to the other side: mission accomplished. Now let's transfer this image to the strategy for combating climate change (which, of course, is infinitely more complicated). According to scientists, the first thing to do is to stop the stream of carbon emissions in order to reach a balance of zero as soon as possible, preferably by 2030; without this, any other strategy is doomed to failure. It would be overwhelmed, much like our explorers on the riverbank, by the power of the greenhouse effect caused by rising concentrations of CO_2. As Greta has pointed out: 'We have to leave fossil fuels where they are: in the ground.'

Once the flow has been tamed, the bridge strategy should be implemented immediately, one stone after another. Once we have sought, found and prepared the right stones, it needs to be done soon – if we stop using fossil fuels we will need alternatives very quickly. In this case, the bridge would be the United Nations' sustainable development agenda and the stones are the individual actions to achieve the plan's objectives: investing in the implementation of renewable energy sources; reducing consumption and the production of polluting waste; recycling; protecting the marine environment; developing sustainable methods of agriculture and animal-rearing; changing our eating habits; and fighting poverty – to name but a few. Only by building a solid bridge with all these stones can the nations of the world finish the task.

Science has now asserted in every language on Earth that this is the only possible way forward, so the next question is: who is dealing with it? Who will block the flow and collect the stones needed to get everyone to the other side safe and sound? According to the IPCC, 'International cooperation is a critical enabler ... [with] industry, civil society and scientific institutions.' So what does this actually mean?

International cooperation is the leadership without which nothing can happen. Countries must find ways to support one another in pursuing this common goal. The developed countries must help their developing counterparts to cut emissions without falling behind in their socio-economic growth, which will cause additional problems to domestic and global equilibrium alike. The worlds of finance and research, both public and private, will have to think in terms of the good of the international community, not of single nations or individual investors. Only by working together will we manage to block the torrent and build the bridge.

Civil society? This means us. We are citizens of a world that is falling ill, a world of people who have left it very late to start thinking we should perhaps find a way of escaping to the other riverbank, but luckily also a world of millions of young people who have raised their voices in response to Greta's global call. It would be fantastic if this new generation were to put into practice – and teach adults – what is required in everyday life to reach the other bank in safety. They have already started: the hashtag #MyClimateAction features in thousands of tweets, Instagram stories and Facebook posts with initiatives, ideas and tricks to promote sustainable development.

Science, technological innovation and industry are the other key ingredients. Scientists must continue to study methods, reliably project results and point the way for governments, investors and citizens. Industry must put the interests of the planet ahead of any personal concerns. Greta has been crystal clear in underlining this point: 'Our biosphere is being sacrificed so that rich people in countries like mine can live in luxury. It is the sufferings of the many which pay for the luxuries of the few. ... We need to focus on equity.'

CHAPTER 7

FOSSIL FUELS

THE ENERGY
WE NEED TO REPLACE

If this were a murder mystery, it would be one of those books where you know the identity of the killer from the start. Fossil fuels have always been in the frame for the greenhouse effect, and therefore also the prime suspect for climate change linked to global warming. There is hardly anybody left who will tell you otherwise, as science now has more than half a century of data to prove the guilt of fossil fuels. The amount of carbon dioxide in the atmosphere is increasing – and continues to do so – in proportion to the burning of organic fossil compounds: coal, oil and natural gas.

In the late 1700s the first British factory owners discovered that burning coal released so much energy that it could power machinery to do the work of hundreds of men; the Industrial Revolution had begun. If you know the stories and films set in the London of that era, you'll know why the fogs were called 'London particulars' or 'pea-soupers' – the smog was so thick you couldn't see your hand in front of your face (pea soup is very thick!). The volumes of coal burned at the time had immediately obvious effects, not only turning the air around those pioneering British factories a dark grey but also staining even the solemn walls of London's Buckingham Palace with the particles released (in addition to CO_2) by combustion, so-called fine and ultra-fine particulate matter. Similar effects have also been observed, in different proportions over the centuries, as a result of burning oil after World War II and also from burning natural gas.

We tend to associate fossil fuels with the things they power today, from the fuel used to make aeroplanes fly to the manufacture of synthetic materials such as plastics. However, they are sourced from deposits of organic material – plants and animals, in other words – that have formed over hundreds of millions of years through decomposition, pressure and heating processes beneath the Earth's crust. The main substances are oil, coal and gas, and together, these make up some 85 percent of the world's energy sources.

When these are burned, the main catalyst of the greenhouse effect, carbon dioxide, is released into the air. Every year, we generate about 21.5 billion tonnes. The natural dispersal system for carbon dioxide, the ancient forests, can absorb only about half of this. This means that every twelve months, we are accumulating 10.75 billion tonnes of CO_2 that will, very efficiently, trap heat on Earth. This is why stopping the craziness of fossil fuel emissions is the first emergency measure to take, as any scientist will tell you; the famous handbrake that Greta wants the people at the top to apply without needing to be told twice.

Although the problem seems simple, it is anything but. Think of any human activity: transport, construction, roads, hospitals, agriculture, fishing, food preservation, industry – from energy production to the factory that built the bicycle you rode to school – extracting drinking water and piping it to our houses, waste recycling: every enterprise that keeps society going depends on the use of energy. Our everyday existence has taken us hostage.

How can we escape? The time for negotiation has now passed. We need robust action, and this must be taken by our leaders. With coordinated intervention across the world, we can invert the proportions of energy coming from non-renewable sources (in other words fossil fuels) and energy from renewable sources plus new sources that have been investigated in recent years: energy sources that release no CO_2 into the atmosphere. Scientists hold a range of different opinions on the role that nuclear energy, which is not renewable, might play in this 'handbrake' phase for fossil fuels; it comes with a host of safety concerns.

China, which still leads the world for emission levels, has already achieved great results; thanks to investment in new energy sources and a stringent national strategy for reducing CO_2, it managed to shrink output of PM2.5 (the fine particles that are released with carbon dioxide when fossil fuels are burned) by 30 percent between 2013 and 2016. It is the largest nation to have complied with the commitments set out in the Paris Agreement, in some cases in advance of deadlines. By contrast, the second-largest producer of carbon dioxide, the United States (whose population, a mere 5 percent of the global total, produces 15 percent of the world's emissions), withdrew from the agreement in 2017.

CHAPTER 8

CLEAN RENEWABLE ENERGY

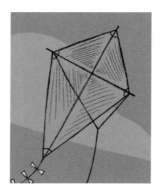

THE SUPERHEROES WHO WILL SAVE THE FUTURE OF THE PLANET

Let's pretend we got rid of fossil fuels. What do we do now? How shall we continue to live, thrive, survive, and help those who need to grow their own economies? Fortunately, fossil fuels are not the only source of energy available: we have sun, wind, water and the heat that rises from the depths of the Earth; we have sources of clean, renewable energy.

According to the IPCC, renewable energy sources should be able to meet between 70 and 85 percent of global energy requirements by 2050. (At the moment, the figure for renewable energy stands at no more than 23 percent.) There are more than six thousand scientific studies suggesting that we can reach the higher figures. Some have different blends of energy sources and solutions and the scenarios may vary (predicting the future is far from easy!), but they all agree on one thing: the greater the growth in renewable energy sources, the better the state of the world and the more help will be given to the poorest countries, who face uncertainty because they don't have reliable sources of energy. It might seem far-fetched to us, as we check our smartphones one more time, but there are still 1.4 billion people in the world with no access to electricity. Try to imagine how they manage everyday tasks such as washing, cooking, reading or pumping drinking water from underground.

Traditional power plants produce large amounts of energy, but they are expensive and are often built close to large towns or cities. The new technologies associated with renewable energy allow us to take action against the principal cause of climate change and at the same time to develop the ability of remote rural areas or entire countries to access secure and independent sources of energy. Research into technologies that are increasingly lightweight, more effective and more efficient will enable this to happen. Investment in these sectors not only improves air quality but also promotes sustainable development. In addition to the classic renewable sources, science is also exploring new, emission-free ways of turning matter into energy, with extraordinary results. Techniques offering the most promising – and above all, green – results include water electrolysis (when a current is passed through water, splitting it into hydrogen and oxygen).

WHAT ARE THE CLASSIC CLEAN RENEWABLE ENERGY SOURCES?

Geothermal energy. This is extracted from heat produced deep within our planet. It is generally captured and used to heat or cool, but it can also be used to generate electricity. The first geothermal energy generator was tested in Larderello, Italy, in July 1904, but California is now one of the leaders in the exploitation of this form of energy. Countries that currently draw more than 15 percent of their energy needs from geothermal sources include Iceland, Costa Rica, the Philippines, El Salvador, Kenya and New Zealand.

Hydroelectric energy. This is generated by the movement of water, either flowing or falling from a height. It can be collected from rivers or generated by constructing dams through which water accumulates at two different levels. It is now used mainly to generate electricity, but was once used to do mechanical work (such as in water mills for grinding wheat into flour). The city of Niagara Falls was lit as early as 1881 with energy generated by the power of the famous waterfalls in North America. Hydroelectric power is the main source of renewable energy (70 percent) and already meets 17 percent of global energy requirements.

Solar energy. Sunlight captured with photovoltaic technology (panels usually installed on the roofs of houses or factories, or on large surfaces) is focused and transformed into electricity. Solar energy has great potential as the structures required are not difficult to install, even on small surfaces, and could bring social and economic benefits to remote areas. There is one problem still to be resolved, however, that of storage, so reserves of energy can be accumulated. The best scientists in the world, from Europe to Asia, are working on the most effective way to maintain constant levels of enough power to meet our needs. The first photovoltaic solar panel was exhibited in Paris in 1878, but was not a success; coal was the preferred energy source at that time.

Wind energy. The kinetic energy (energy produced by motion) of air can be turned into electricity using large turbines, and wind farms capable of capturing air flow have been built on land and in the middle of the sea. The technique generates no emissions but, much like solar power systems, has to contend with changes in the weather, and improvement is needed in the technologies used to store energy over longer periods of time. Wind power, which currently supplies 4.4 percent of the energy used around the world, is booming and is considered one of the sources with the greatest potential.

Marine energy. As with wind, the kinetic energy of sea currents is captured with turbines that transform it into electricity. Energy can also be extracted from our seas and oceans via wave motion and the differences in the chemical composition of water. Many projects underway in this sector are still to be finalized; while the technique produces no emissions, it may have detrimental effects on marine habitats.

CHAPTER 9

DRINKING WATER

TECHNOLOGY TO SAVE
TWO BILLION PEOPLE

Is drinking water the new oil? This question has been posed variously by the *Financial Times*, by long-term investment managers from major international banks and by legislators, and many global companies have been purchasing sources of the precious liquid over the past decade. Even the Bush family, the sons of the former president of the United States, have got out their chequebooks to buy access rights to the Guarani Aquifer, one of the largest aquifers (a layer of rock that stores water) in the world, which flows beneath the soil of Paraguay, Brazil, Uruguay and Argentina. *Follow the money*, as they say. When large investments are being made, it means that something is interesting to the markets, and demand for that particular asset will go higher and higher. The problem in this case is that the demand is called thirst.

Water covers 70 percent of the planet's surface (the same percentage as our bodies contain), but only a small fraction of this is drinkable. In theory, there is enough for everyone, but there are two main problems: governments that are inefficient in making it accessible, and climate change. With international cooperation, the percentage of the world's population with access to a source of drinking water increased from 70 to 90 percent in fifteen years (1990–2005). However, the World Health Organization states there are currently more than two billion people in the world who have none. This incredibly high figure includes 263 million people (mostly women and children) who must walk for hours every day to reach the nearest source of water to their home. All this has a cost, not only in terms of the lives it claims (361,000 children under the age of five die every year from diseases related to drinking contaminated water) but also in its social and economic fallout: women and children spend most of their day walking to wells to ensure the survival of the family rather than studying or working. Lack of drinking water is one of the key points on the agenda for sustainable development. If it can be resolved, other fundamental issues will follow in turn: education, better lives and more freedom for women, security and the fight against poverty.

According to the IPCC, climate change is already affecting access to global water resources, both in terms of the quantity and quality of the drinking water available. Melting of permanent ice cover is upsetting the hydrogeological equilibrium (balance of water underground) of major regions of the planet, with disastrous consequences for the surrounding areas. Rainy seasons and precipitation (rainfall) patterns have already changed in frequency and intensity, bringing dry seasons or sudden flooding to areas once far more securely balanced. Other regions, already vulnerable as a result of difficult social and economic conditions, have now become dependent on external aid to survive their chronic water shortages. In addition to the climate, poor government of the areas worst affected is causing thirst and disease. In the absence of adequate water management, for example, even the water sources available will soon become polluted and therefore unusable or actively harmful. We need proper monitoring, rigorous control and transparent investment. The United Nations has a target of access to safe drinking water for everyone by 2030, working extensively in areas such as Africa and Central, South and Southeast Asia.

Science and the development of clean energy sources may once again come to the rescue, in the first instance by mitigating the effects of the climate change that is already underway and helping to cut emissions, as we have learned. In the meantime, however, they could also solve the problem of adapting to change and help people to live better lives right now. A beautiful story called *The Boy Who Harnessed the Wind* has been turned into a film recounting how teenager William Kamkwamba saved his village in Malawi from famine caused by an alternation of flooding (the result in part of brutal deforestation) and drought. He built a windmill from parts of his father's bicycle, a dynamo and old car batteries. Using just this one small wind vane, he was able to generate enough energy to pump water from underground, irrigating part of a field and growing enough to feed about twenty people, the inhabitants left in the village from which many had fled. After his story went viral thanks to a TED Talk (the same programme for sharing innovative ideas that played host to Greta), William was able to study environmental engineering in the United States and now plans to rid his land of water shortages by constructing small solar energy and wind power stations in villages. *Time* magazine has included his name in its '30 Under 30' list of the world's most influential young people.

CHAPTER 10

WASTE AND RECYCLING

OUR RUBBISH IS HELPING TO RAISE THE TEMPERATURE OF THE PLANET

'You say you love your children above all else, yet you are stealing their future in front of their very eyes,' Greta reminded world leaders (and adults in general). The numbers speak for themselves: according to a UNICEF report submitted in October 2016, one child in seven around the world is breathing toxic air that is contaminated with fine dust, dioxins, sulphur dioxide and more. 'The world community should minimize exposure to pollutants as soon as possible,' Anthony Lake, the Executive Director of UNICEF (the United Nations Children's Fund) until 2017, has said. Fossil fuels and toxic gases from waste management are at the top of the list. What links this emergency to climate change?

The term 'waste management' crops up frequently in reports on climate change, but at first sight the connection may not seem that straightforward. Take a moment to think, however, and it becomes obvious: an enormous amount of energy has been used to manufacture the things we throw away. To make the can from which you have just finished drinking, aluminium was extracted from a mine, perhaps in Australia, and then processed in a series of different stages until it was can-shaped. The can was then transported, probably by ship or plane, to a factory thousands of miles away, where it was filled with your favourite beverage. Another means of transport brought it to the supermarket or your local bar. In throwing away that can, you have helped to increase the level of carbon dioxide in the air, and thereby to escalate climate change, in proportion to the quantities of energy used to make all this possible.

The quantities of energy used: this is the key. How can we use less energy to make the can from which you drink next time? The IPCC has confirmed that primary production of an object uses four to five times as much energy as secondary manufacturing. Primary production is making something from materials extracted from their original source (for example cutting trees to make paper); secondary manufacturing is when the item is created from recycled materials. For aluminium, whose extraction costs are extremely high in energy, this ratio rises to 1:40 – producing one tonne of aluminium by extracting it from the ground uses forty times the energy required to produce the same tonne from recycled aluminium.

Recycling is therefore one of the most important ways to help counter the effects of climate change, although consuming less overall is still the number one way we can help. Greater consumption means higher energy use in sourcing the raw materials, producing the goods and transporting them to markets all over the world (no doubt wrapped up in nice packaging that in turn has undergone the same manufacturing process, with a proportionate cost in energy). In addition, everything we throw away (unless properly sorted and recycled) represents a further emission of considerable quantities of gases that include methane, an element produced from the decay of organic waste that has an even greater greenhouse effect than carbon dioxide.

The problem with waste, unfortunately, is that it can release other highly toxic elements, in addition to methane, into the air and water if appropriate precautions are not taken. Per capita consumption (the amount consumed by each citizen) has been increasing in developed countries and mass consumption has risen sharply in developing countries. It builds up rapidly around cities that in a few years will be populated by millions of people – who in turn will produce enormous quantities of waste. While some of the larger emerging countries (foremost among them China and India) are investing heavily in attempts to address this emergency in a technologically appropriate way, other countries are falling behind, and vast regions are bearing the brunt of the large quantities of harmful emissions generated in the manufacture and disposal of products. Together with Africa, South and Southeast Asia are the worst affected regions.

CHAPTER 11

PLASTIC

THE INVISIBLE KILLER
WE CAN STOP

Drinking straws, cotton buds, cutlery, plates, glasses, even sticks for balloons – all these disposable plastic products (which account for more than 70 percent of the trash found on beaches) will be banned in the countries of the European Union from 2021. By 2029, 90 percent of plastic bottles will have to be returned to the manufacturer via a deposit system similar to those already in use for glass bottles. Europe is making a move towards reducing the prime pollutant of marine systems (and thus of the planet in general): plastic.

This extremely flexible material was invented seventy years ago and has revolutionized the way the entire population of the world lives. It enabled the manufacture of items (in whole or in part) that have become essential to the growth of society, from food packaging (allowing food to be shipped in hygienic and stable conditions) to modes of transport that are available to all. Plastic and oil (plastic is manufactured from oil) have opened up the industrial potential of Western countries and both have contributed to the boom in these economies. These days, eight million tonnes of plastic is scattered into the oceans every year, with inland waste carried out to sea by the great rivers of the world, above all those in Asia and Africa.

Plastic is the main ingredient of the trash to be found in the sea. We have all seen images of stranded whales with pounds of rubbish in their stomachs, of turtles chasing plastic bags thinking they were food, of birds feeding their young small pieces of plastic, mistaking them for brightly coloured life forms – and instead resulting in the premature death of their offspring. Beaches scattered with litter attract thousands of young people organized by the #cleanthebeach social media campaign, while the enormous island of garbage, mostly plastic, which is forming in a swirl of currents between California and Hawaii, has grown to three times the size of France. But this is only the tip of the iceberg.

Even if we cleaned up every single piece of plastic visible to the naked eye, the most dangerous part would still be left as a pollutant. Plastic does not decompose upon exposure to sunlight; instead, it fragments into tiny particles that scientists call micro- and nano-plastics. Humans sometimes manufacture plastics this small and include them in products such as cosmetics; the almost invisible particles are absorbed into running water and enter the sewerage system directly, at the end of which filtration methods are able to capture no more than 90 percent. The remainder not only cause pollution but can attract chemical or bacterial contaminants, heavy metals and other substances that, once carried into the food chain (such plastics are about the same size as plankton) can result in health problems that are as serious for marine creatures as they are for humans.

In addition to recently passed legislation, the good news is that we as individuals have the power to reduce our consumption of plastic. We can do this by recycling, of course, but more than anything, by using as little as possible. We can, for example, ask about the quality of the drinking water in our area and, having filtered it (hundreds of filters are available), drink water from the tap rather than from bottles. We can choose to buy plastic-free products and use things made from biodegradable materials. Try to do your shopping in one of the many 'zero packaging' outlets around the world, and to buy products in bulk, which saves packaging.

CHAPTER 12

BIODIVERSITY

FROM POLE TO POLE, WE ARE ALL FELLOW TRAVELLERS ON EARTH

Another powerful voice was raised to join young Greta's before an assembly of politicians and economists at the World Economic Forum, and it quickly went around the globe. It belonged to ninety-two-year-old Sir David Attenborough, author and natural history documentary-maker, who has been talking for sixty years about 'the wonderful creatures with which we share our planet'. Sir David has always fought to draw attention to the damage and risks to which 'biodiversity' is exposed – a unique word to define all our fellow passengers on this precious ship, the Earth.

'I am quite literally from another age,' he reminded Davos. 'I was born during the Holocene, the name given to the 12,000-year period of climatic stability that allowed humans to settle, farm and create civilizations. ... Now, in the space of one human lifetime, indeed in the space of *my* lifetime, all that has changed: the Holocene has ended. ... We have changed the world so much that scientists say we are now in a new geological age – the Anthropocene – the Age of Humans.' But now, 'we have to come together as humans to save biodiversity. No one can do it alone because we live in a unique system, we are all linked in making key choices to combat climate change. How we act now will have profound effects that will have repercussions for millennia to come.'

The consequences of climate change for biodiversity were addressed in the fifth IPCC Synthesis Report (AR5), which concluded: 'A large fraction of terrestrial, freshwater and marine species faces increased extinction risk' in the climate change scenario anticipated. Preserving terrestrial ecosystems on land, in the oceans and in our fresh watercourses, is essential for the survival of all species, including our own. The Amazon rainforest, for example, is a treasure trove of biodiversity, with many hundreds of thousands of species yet to be discovered and recorded; it represents one of the main natural means of controlling carbon dioxide emissions, thanks to the filtering capabilities of its greenery. Failing to protect it by allowing deforestation to continue means prolonging the threat to this special ecosystem and missing the opportunity to reduce a significant portion of the CO_2 present in the atmosphere, a vital step in slowing the pace of global warming.

In fact, the regions where the effects of climate change on the ecosystem are being felt most evidently are the Arctic, the Great Barrier Reef off the coast of Australia and the Amazon. An area that has been degraded – stripped of its flora and fauna – is also an area that is more vulnerable. Take the mangroves, which are at risk not only from rising sea levels but also from the exploitation of coastal areas for industrial and commercial ends. With their imposing structure of trunks ranged along the shore atop a solid tangle of underwater roots, these plants protect the coastal populations of the Pacific, South America and equatorial Africa from the effects of the flooding and storms that are now becoming increasingly frequent, and they guarantee the equilibrium of the ecosystem, providing shelter and nourishment for fish species that have always been the basis of local economies. Losing these literally means giving up oxygen, both in the air and in society.

The melting of glaciers is also threatening the habitat and survival of many species; the case of polar bears is well known, with some forced to swim for excessive distances to find a floe of solid ice, and others who have grave difficulties in hunting for themselves and their cubs. Warming of the oceans has also resulted in coral bleaching, the progressive death of coral reefs, which lose their coloration once their vitality is lost. Changes in air current temperatures and rainfall have an additional effect because they interfere with annual and periodic events that are typical of some species, such as bird migration.

Preserving biodiversity also means researching it. How can we protect something we do not understand? Many studies in this field are undertaken thanks to the enthusiasm of countries such as Australia and New Zealand, which consider biodiversity 'added value of national importance' and are investing millions of dollars in a joint study that seeks to map all the species on their land mass, including tens of thousands yet to be discovered. Knowing, as Sir David Attenborough hopes, will make us understand better and follow a wiser path in this new era.

CHAPTER 13

MAKING AGRICULTURE, ANIMAL-REARING AND FISHING SUSTAINABLE

WASTE LESS, PRODUCE MORE AND PROTECT THE LAND TO FEED THE WORLD

If we want to feed a population set to reach 9.3 billion people by 2050 – two billion more than today – scientists think we will have to reimagine the global agricultural industry in terms of its efficiency and its conservation of the ecosystem. To combat hunger, we will have to increase production by 60 percent globally, and double the output of developing countries.

According to the United Nations' Food and Agriculture Organization (FAO), an average of 23.7 million tonnes of food is produced daily worldwide, including 19.5 million tonnes of cereals, root crops, tubers, fruit and vegetables; 1.1 million tonnes of meat; and 2.1 billion litres of milk. Some 400,000 tonnes of fish are trawled daily from the sea or produced in fish farms. 9.5 million cubic metres of wood are chopped down from the forests and on that very same average day, no fewer than 7.4 trillion (thousand million) litres of water are used to irrigate cultivated fields, with 300,000 tonnes of fertilizer dumped on top. The total value of this average day of agri-food production has been estimated by the FAO at approaching US$7 billion, and the sector employs one third of the world's workforce.

These are impressive figures, but beyond all this, agriculture, animal husbandry and fishing play a fundamental role in rural areas and smaller coastal regions by keeping communities together and nurturing local culture. Many oral story-telling traditions are inspired by epic tales of drought or famine, floods or storms, and their narrative power lies in descriptions of how a particular character manages to save entire villages or boat crews from apocalyptic threats. Food production is as much a part of human culture as our ability to tell stories.

What can we do to double food production and adhere to our goals for cutting emissions? In addition to changing our diets, we will certainly have to reduce food waste and invest in technologies that minimize the environmental impact of producing food – saving water, for example, by calculating exactly how much is needed for irrigation based on swiftly changing variables such as wind, humidity and hours of sunlight. There is a steady increase in the number of patents for drone-related apps in the United States, and these are being used to monitor entire crops and farms, providing and processing useful data so that production can be more accurately managed and wastage of both drinking water and energy reduced. The United Nations' agenda for sustainable development anticipates investing in resilient cultivation systems to combat food shortages in developing countries by 2030. This will mean not only that agriculture and animal-rearing will have to become more efficient (in other words produce more from a given amount of land) but also that the original ecosystem must be maintained because it will help the land respond to the effects of climate change. Sustainable agriculture is at the heart of the struggle to end world hunger and save the planet.

The FAO oversees long-standing programmes to address sustainability in a range of sectors, including agriculture, livestock breeding and fishing. As the last report has emphasized, the time has now come to make every country and sector work together on an integrated approach to mutual sustainability. What does that mean? It means we must pass international legislation that prevents farming from wiping out a region's ecosystem, as happens periodically in the forests of Indonesia as a result of the market for palm oil fruit.

It means that we must allow fish stocks to replenish themselves, as already happens in the Mediterranean, while also allowing local communities to carry on fishing to support themselves, by traditional methods and on a small commercial scale. It means that caring for our land and oceans, preventing pollution and looking after our woods and forests is not merely enforced by legislation but carried out in the interests of individuals wishing to live in safe, viable regions. In essence, it means starting to think in terms of what will bring benefit to all, not just to individuals.

CHAPTER 14

THE DIET THAT WILL HEAL THE PLANET

PLENTY OF FRUIT, VEGETABLES AND LEGUMES, BUT WITHOUT GIVING ANYTHING UP

———

We know what is required for a drastic reduction in the production of red meat (especially beef and lamb), the average cost of which is twenty times greater in terms of emissions and land use than producing other forms of protein (such as vegetable protein). Radical reform of agriculture and animal husbandry and a rethinking of our diets are identified by the IPCC as necessary to achieve the goal of limiting global warming to +1.5°C. We will have to eat less red meat and also prevent large-scale animal farming from continuing to cut down immense swathes of forest at an ever-increasing rate. Saving forests means saving their ability to absorb the carbon dioxide present in the atmosphere. According to the IPCC, we should therefore immediately restrict the demand for food whose production increases CO_2 emissions, and nudge the world towards a healthier and more sustainable diet – a notion that goes hand in hand with the advice, widely offered, to consume seasonal and local food to avoid the cost (in terms of emissions) of transporting, say, a strawberry in November, or shipping a pint of Australian milk to Beijing.

There is good news: to save the planet, we will not be required to give up our favourite foods forever (unless you are a fan of shark fin soup, of course). A recent study published in the scientific journal *The Lancet* identified a diet that could limit climate change and contribute to sustainable development if eaten by the majority of the world's population. The 37 scientists who make up the EAT-Lancet Commission have dubbed it the 'planetary health diet' and it could help to save 11.6 million lives per year while at the same time assisting in achieving the goals set out in the Paris Agreement. It suggests restricting consumption of sugar and red meat as much as possible while doubling intakes of fruit, vegetables, legumes (beans, peas, lentils and other pulses), seeds and nuts.

The planetary health diet allows about 2,500 calories per day, balanced across all food groups and calculated for the requirements of the average population. The basic idea is that at least half of our plate should be filled with leafy green vegetables as well as other vegetables and fruit. In addition, we are allowed vegetable proteins (sourced mainly from legumes but also from nuts and seeds), and we do not have to renounce animal produce entirely: dairy products, eggs and meat are permitted in small quantities. Those already following moderately balanced diets will notice its many similarities to what food science already considers the healthiest mix. The planetary health diet recommends consuming up to about 500 g of fruit and vegetables per day (made up of 300 g vegetables and 200 g fruit), combined with 250 g of dairy products (equating to two servings of yoghurt or a glass of milk), 230 g of wholegrain cereals (rice, wheat or others), 75 g of legumes, 50 g of vegetable oil (better than olive oil) and 50 g of nuts. Red meat is allowed in your diet once a week in moderate quantities (approx 100 g), as well as 200 g of fish, 200 g of chicken and 2 eggs.

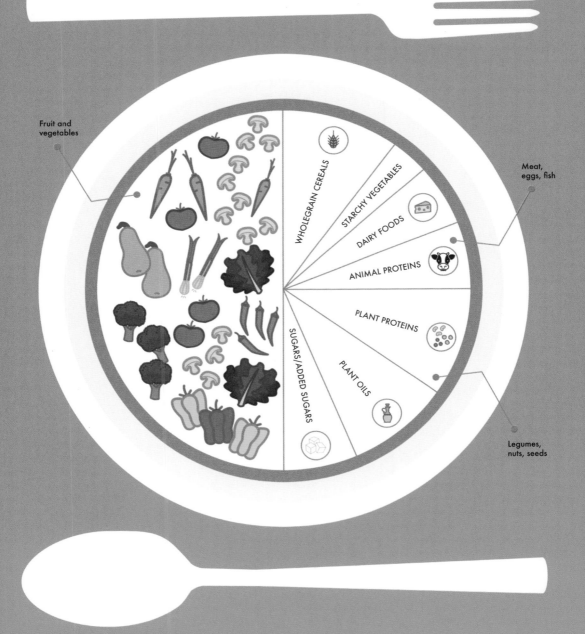

Fruit and
vegetables

Meat,
eggs, fish

Legumes,
nuts, seeds

WHOLEGRAIN CEREALS

STARCHY VEGETABLES

DAIRY FOODS

ANIMAL PROTEINS

PLANT PROTEINS

PLANT OILS

SUGARS/ADDED SUGARS

Source: EAT-Lancet Commission

CHAPTER 15
LIVING IN
CITIES

THE ECOLOGICAL ALTERNATIVE FOR URBAN CENTRES

Over half the world's population lives in cities; in Britain and the USA, more than 80 percent of us do. Making metropolitan life sustainable is an essential challenge for the planet's future, and there is so much scope for improvement.

This might come as a surprise: did you know that city living could potentially be more sustainable and more ecological than life in the country? Potentially, of course – in the sense that living in close proximity to one another can lead to greater energy efficiency and as a result to a significant reduction in emissions. How does that work? It's simple: if I can walk to work, cycle or use an electric public transport system powered from renewable sources, my CO_2 emissions will be zero. If my waste, once I have properly separated it, is sorted and recycled or converted into energy in efficient power plants (like the ones being built in big cities), my contribution to air and water pollution is going to be equally minimal. If I can choose where I want to shop from among many shops, supermarkets and fresh produce markets, I can choose those with zero packaging and food miles, thereby rewarding distributors who want to reduce their impact on the environment. By contrast, if I live miles from centres offering a wide range of services, I will have to content myself with whatever is on offer at the nearest shop or drive to one that suits my needs better, using up energy on private transport.

Cities are important frontiers for ecology in the sense that they harbour enormous potential for implementing the changes needed to achieve a balance of zero emissions. Researchers have been aware of this for decades, with universities leading the way in merging architecture, engineering, chemistry and design to explore new intelligent, ecological cities, the so-called smart cities. One of the things the Senseable City Lab, led by Italian architect Carlo Ratti at Massachusetts Institute of Technology (MIT), is working on is harvesting data from mobile phones to understand the dynamics of city life better. By cross-referencing the data from users who take part in this research, the systems can reconstruct, understand and make use of citizens' travel habits, preferred means of transport, journey times and favourite routes in order to make transport more efficient.

These same phones can even signal the repair status of bridges and other infrastructure, for example, by automatically sending data showing the vibration frequency of the bridge (a parameter that defines how healthy such a structure is) every time you cross it. Being aware of the condition of major infrastructure at all times and at virtually zero cost helps cities to increase safety and also to boost their own resilience (their resistance to the effects of climate change) in an energy-efficient way.

We now know of so many ways for a city to increase its environmental sustainability, the first of which is by expanding its renewable clean energy sources: solar, wind and hydroelectric power can transform a city into a 'zero fossil fuel consumer'. Basel in Switzerland and Burlington, Vermont, in the USA, among many others, have already successfully made this leap (according to data from CDP, the Carbon Disclosure Project, which at the time of writing covers 620 cities around the world and collects information about energy efficiency) and there are more than 100 conurbations on the planet that draw at least 70 percent of their energy from renewable sources. 'Smart' buildings (technologically advanced, efficient and environmentally friendly homes with energy-saving features) make a significant con-tribution in such cases. Their design takes careful account of their relationship with public transport and the rest of the city, and also encourages working from home by making the latest generation of web connections available to residents.

In addition, the most sensitized cities are boosting the ecological networks formed by the natural and semi-natural spaces present within their built-up areas and along watercourses by planting trees and ensuring that at least 20 percent of their area is green space (the percentage considered essential to mitigate the rise in warming caused by the greater surface area of cement and asphalt in urban centres). London, for example, has long nurtured its ecological networks and biodiversity, becoming the world's first National Park City in July 2019. It is also of key importance to allow space for small businesses within urban agriculture, making use of communal areas and also encouraging the use of private spaces for hydroponic (growing without soil, using only water) cultivation of vegetables to meet food quotas with zero food miles.

It is equally vital to organize public transport systems as a priority within cities and to expand pedestrian areas and extend cycle routes. Concentration of services and workplaces in a single centre must be avoided and a widespread network created across the entire area, allowing for the distance between where you work and where you live to be kept to a minimum (one of the ways to do this is to encourage working from home). Thousands of cities in countries across the world, from Australia to Brazil, are now heading in this direction and have created websites on which they share their experiences and outcomes. One of the most authoritative is Climate-ADAPT, which was born of a partnership between the European Commission and the European Environment Agency (EEA).

CHAPTER 16

THE KEYS TO THE
FUTURE

IDEAS AND RESEARCH
FOR A BETTER WORLD

On 1 July 1979, Mr Sony (whose birth name was Masaru Ibuka) launched a small box on the market that could play tapes through headphones. At the time, no one could have predicted that the 'Walkman' would revolutionize not only the way we listened to music but also the daily life of millions of young people. Such is the power of inventions, especially Japanese ones! It's no surprise that one of the most interesting initiatives in the field of renewable energy sources comes from that region: Tokyo wants to be the first city to supply the Olympic Games (in 2020) with energy sourced from hydrogen. And not just as fuel for vehicles (a system that has already been tested by local car manufacturers and is used in the national public transport network), but also in other applications, such as energy supply to buildings. Keen to distance itself from the 2011 nuclear disaster at Fukushima by seeking safer and greener alternatives, Japan is still using raw materials such as methane for the production of hydrogen energy, but in the near future, there is every chance of developing new technologies that permit the electrolysis of water, splitting it into hydrogen and oxygen in a zero-emission process. Improvements still need to be made to the concept, but researchers foresee a short development period, benefiting both the economy and the environment.

Ideas that benefit the planet don't have to come from major invest-ments, however, whether public or private. Sometimes you need to listen to small entrepreneurs from around the world, often young people dreaming up ingenious solutions to problems. One such is Scott Munguía, a Mexican engineering student who invented an entirely natural plastic by recycling avocado stones (the fruit is one of his country's top exports). Another is Freight Farms, a Boston start-up that sells shipping containers for use as mini hydroponic farms. Food can be grown in the container on a small plot of land – even in a car park – and the food can be sold locally too, with zero food miles.

Our universities have also become incubators of innovative green ideas – such as the laboratory headed by Francesco Ciucci from Ravenna in Italy, who is Associate Professor of Aerospace Engineering at the Hong Kong University of Science and Technology. His research involves young graduate students from around the world, and is following cutting-edge trends in energy storage with the aim of reducing the environmental impact of batteries. We often don't realize just how many potentially toxic elements (lithium, lead, cobalt and electrolytes, to name but a few) lurk hidden within the items in daily use to power our laptops, phones and cars.

The problem of capturing and storing energy for use when required has become increasingly pressing over recent years. Renewable energy sources have the potential to free entire sectors from energy dependency (the electric car could quickly make the internal combustion engine obsolete and reduce CO_2 emissions accordingly), but the systems for energy retention and storage will have to become more efficient and reduce their environmental impact. Ciucci's laboratory is working in cooperation with the world's leading public and private research institutions from Japan to Germany on the development of a technology that promises to revolutionize the road transport industry: the solid-state battery. Such systems use ceramic materials and are much more ecological and compact than chemical batteries, but they are still too heavy. Despite this, it has been esti-mated that the first electric cars fitted with this type of battery could be in production within five years, extending the range achievable with a single charge from the current 400 km (250 miles) to almost double that. There may still be some way to go, but there is no lack of enthusiasm to achieve this change.

CHAPTER 17

#MY CLIMATE ACTION

TEN SMALL THINGS WE CAN DO TO MAKE A DIFFERENCE

No man is an island. Everything we do, even the smallest gesture, can make a difference. This is not just an expression, it is a scientific fact: sociological research has shown that when a person or a group does the right thing, others tend to follow suit. How about a few examples? A newspaper featuring an article with the headline 'One American in three has stopped eating red meat' was left on tables for customers to read in an American diner; orders for red meat fell by 30 percent in the restaurant that day. Or this: installation of solar panels in a neighbourhood triggers a 'copycat' reaction that quickly results in that neighbourhood ending up with a far higher percentage of panels than average. This happens because a part of our brain is dedicated to the important task of evaluating the costs and benefits of other people's actions. If the benefits of sustainable behaviour, such as eating less meat, are perceived to be higher than the costs (giving up steak), we tend to imitate such behaviour.

So here are ten small (big!) actions to start us off in helping to bring about change. Do you have any other suggestions? Write them down, post them, share them, let everyone know – let's make #MyClimateAction a useful hashtag that helps to reduce the planet's temperature.

1. DRINK TAP WATER AND CARRY YOUR OWN BOTTLE

Water from a plastic bottle is almost never better; it is more expensive (not least in terms of the associated emissions of CO_2) and it generates vast amounts of waste. Check the make-up of the mains water where you live: it is controlled by law and guaranteed fit for human consumption. There are also excellent filters on the market that are cheap and easy to install, and these will extract any unwanted substances (such as chlorine) from the water while leaving the essential mineral content untouched. Buy your own personal water bottle, made of aluminium, glass or even plastic as long as you use it for life; this is a very simple way of avoiding having to buy single-use bottles at bars, at the office or on the street.

2. WASTE NO WATER

Let's take quick showers, running the water for only as long as really required, and fit shower heads that reduce water use. We can use natural detergents such as vinegar to wash surfaces and floors; these need a minimum of rinsing, release no harmful substances and, most importantly, do not come in a plastic bottle like most of the chemical cleaners available in the shops.

3. REDISCOVER BARS OF SOAP

Remember bars of soap? They still exist. We don't need plastic bottles with a dispenser nozzle to wash our hands or take a shower. You can also buy shampoo in solid blocks, which reduces plastic waste. Take a quick look online and you will be spoiled for choice.

4. GIVE BAMBOO A TRY TOO

Bamboo is waterproof, light and hygienic and lends itself to a thousand uses for tasks involving contact with water: toothbrushes, hairbrushes, cutlery, plates and shatterproof beakers for children.

5. LET'S ALL GO ON A PLASTIC-FREE PICNIC (WITH NO WASTE)

Plastic glasses and cutlery are top of the list of rubbish that ends up in the sea forever. By 2021 they will be outlawed in Europe. All you need for a picnic is a basket that will take all your plates and dishes and is made out of other materials (metal, wood, bamboo – see above). Take it home at the end of the day and if there are lots of you, each person can carry their own.

6. WALK, CYCLE AND USE PUBLIC TRANSPORT

The obvious idea for reducing emissions is to leave the car at home as often as possible. There are electric car-sharing schemes (in big cities, at least), public transport, weekend rental schemes and cycle paths. And if these options aren't yet available in your area, ask for them.

7. STORE FOOD IN GLASS AND CERAMICS

Remember Grandma's fridge, with leftovers from lunch covered with a plate? There's nothing wrong with this method of saving food, so let's use it! Forget clingfilm, moulded lids and plastic containers: glass and ceramics are fine and don't need to be thrown away after one use.

8. BE SWITCHED ON ABOUT TURNING OFF LIGHTS AND AIR-CONDITIONING

Low-energy lightbulbs are a given, but we should also be turning on fewer lights. You can't be everywhere at once, so remember to turn off the lights when you leave a room. And let's use air-conditioning only when it is absolutely essential.

9. CULTIVATE YOUR GARDEN

Whether your little patch is hydroponic or traditional, down the back garden or up on the balcony, why not grow some vegetables? It's a fantastic way of increasing the proportion of your diet with zero food miles, while making your city greener. Gardening is also a great way of unwinding from stress for those who give it a go.

10. EXPLORE THE RECYCLING CENTRE

Every town has its own waste disposal system, but understanding how recycling works can sometimes be more difficult than deciphering a code from outer space. Why not take a tour with the manager, ask for clear information and share it with neighbours. Remember the copycat principle? It works.

CHAPTER 18

KEY WORDS AND SITES

UNDERSTANDING THE CLIMATE CHALLENGE: USEFUL WORDS

Anthropogenic: caused by human activity.

Biodiversity: the variety of living organisms present in an area.

Biosphere: all living organisms.

Civil society: the set of social, cultural and economic relationships that exist between the citizens of a nation.

Climate change: variation in average climate conditions or changes (discounting extreme events) persisting for an extended period (thirty years or more).

Coral bleaching: a whitening and loss of life observed in coral reefs due to various environmental factors, including a rise in average sea temperatures.

Ecology: how organisms (from animals to single cells) relate to each other and with their surroundings.

Ecosystem: the interaction of living organisms present in an area, both among themselves and with the surrounding environment.

Fossil fuels: organic substances formed underground millions of years ago. They include oil, coal and natural gas. When burned, they produce energy and carbon dioxide. According to some studies, we are nearly halfway through all our reserves of fossil fuels.

#FridaysForFuture: a global student movement launched in 270 countries at the end of 2018 to draw the attention of world leaders and society at large to the effects of climate change. The movement was born as a result of the speeches made by Greta Thunberg, a young environmental activist from Sweden.

Global warming: the increase in average temperature of the planet that is attributable to the greenhouse effect, principally caused by carbon dioxide emissions.

Greenhouse effect: when carbon dioxide, other gases and water vapour allow radiation from the sun to enter the atmosphere but trap the warmth emanating from the Earth, heating the planet's surface and atmosphere.

International cooperation: a form of collaboration between nation states to develop areas in emerging countries that are vulnerable from an economic, social or environmental point of view.

Renewable energy sources: sources of energy from the light of the sun (solar power), wind power, water (hydroelectric power) or geothermal heat.

Resilience: the ability of a state or area to combat natural disasters and phenomena.

#SchoolStrikeForClimate: a strike organized by students around the world who, instead of going into their classrooms, demonstrate in front of their government buildings every Friday morning to demand concrete action against climate change. The first #SchoolStrikeForClimate was the one undertaken by Greta Thunberg beginning on 20 August 2018.

Sustainable development: economic development that gives equal opportunities to all to prosper, and does not harm the environment.

TED: an international platform promoting the circulation of new ideas and opinions both online (TED Talks) and at the conferences it holds in cities around the world.

Waste management: operation of all the processes to deal with waste, from production to disposal or recycling.

STAYING INFORMED: AUTHORITATIVE WEBSITES

Carbon Disclosure Project: www.cdp.net/en
European Climate Adaptation Platform:
https://climate-adapt.eea.europa.eu
European Environment Agency: www.eea.europa.eu
Food and Agriculture Organization of the United Nations:
http://www.fao.org
Greenpeace: www.greenpeace.org
Greta's speeches: www.fridaysforfuture.org/
greta-speeches
Intergovernmental Panel on Climate Change: www.ipcc.ch
National Aeronautics and Space Administration:
www.nasa.gov
School strikes: www.schoolstrike4climate.com (Australia)
www.campaigncc.org (UK)
www.youthclimatestrikeus.org (USA)
United Nations: www.un.org/en
World Economic Forum: www.weforum.org
World Health Organization: www.who.int
World Wide Fund for Nature: wwf.panda.org

BIBLIOGRAPHY

'AR5 Climate Change 2014: Mitigation of Climate Change', Intergovernmental Panel on Climate Change, *November 2014*.

'Clear the Air for Children', UNICEF Report, *October 2016*.

'The Future of Food and Agriculture: Trends and Challenges', United Nations Food and Agriculture Organization), *2017*.

'The Planetary Health Diet', EAT-Lancet Commission, *January 2019*.

'Special Report: Global Warming of 1.5 °C', Intergovernmental Panel on Climate Change, *October 2018*.

'The Sustainable Development Goals Report 2018', United Nations, New York, *2018*.

'Understanding and acting on the complexity of climate change', Hans Bruyninckx, Executive Director of the European Environment Agency, *September 2018*.

REFERENCES

Selected words from Greta:

TEDx Stockholm, *November 2018.*

COP24 (United Nations Climate Change Conference), Katowice, Poland, *December 2018.*

World Economic Forum, Davos, *January 2019.*

ACKNOWLEDGEMENTS

Thanks are due to Lucia Esther Maruzzelli, co-founder (with Valentina Giannella) of the Mind the Gap agency for in-depth journalism in Hong Kong, for editing the text.

Thanks to Sergio Castellari for his scientific review of climate-related issues. Castellari is a climatologist at the National Institute of Geophysics and Vulcanology (INGV) in Bologna and currently seconded as a national expert to the European Union's European Environment Agency (EEA) in Copenhagen, Denmark; his work addresses in particular issues relating to climate change adaptation and disaster risk reduction.

Thanks to Andrea Filpa for reviewing the section on sustainable cities; Filpa lectures in Urban Design at the Department of Architecture at Roma Tre University and is a member of the scientific committee of WWF Italy. Thanks also to Balthazar Pagani, Manuela Cuoghi, Salvatore Giannella, Francesco Ciucci, Mariapaola Paiola and Alessandro Lucchini.

Thank you, Massimo, Agata and Leonardo.